Where we walk

To Mama with love ~

Christmas 2015 ~

Beth

Where we walk

Poems rooted
in the soil of New England

To

Liz

with warm wishes ~

by Sydney Eddison

Sydney Eddison

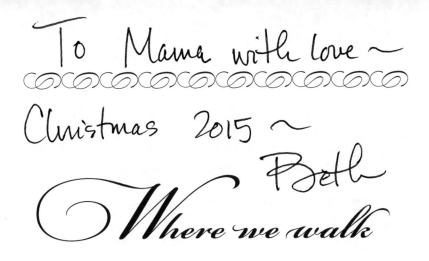

Pomperaug Valley Press
Newtown, Connecticut

For information:
Pomperaug Valley Press
65 Echo Valley Road
Newtown, CT 06470

ISBN-10: 1514807343
ISBN-13: 9781514807347

First printing: July 2015
Printed in the United States of America

Editor: Lorraine Anderson
Front and back cover photos: © 2015 Kimberly Day Proctor
Cover and interior design: Barbara Cottingham

Printed by CreateSpace

Also by Sydney Eddison

A Patchwork Garden: Unexpected Pleasures from a Country Garden (1990)

A Passion for Daylilies: The Flowers and the People (1993)

The Unsung Season: Gardens and Gardeners in Winter (1995)

The Self-Taught Gardener: Lessons from a Country Garden (1997)

The Gardener's Palette: Creating Color in the Garden (2003)

Gardens to Go: Creating and Designing a Container Garden (2005)

Gardening for a Lifetime: How to Garden Wiser as You Grow Older (2010)

Table of Contents

The Garden Year 57

Love, Loss, and Moving On 83

Preface

$\mathcal{G}$rowing up in rural Connecticut in the late nineteen thirties and early forties, my younger brother and I had almost unlimited freedom. Our older brother was already in high school, and both our parents were busy and preoccupied with the Second World War. Our father was an overworked doctor, and our English mother, deeply involved in British war relief. Mamie, a middle-aged woman with no education but a kind heart fed us and kept house, while Hugh and I escaped into the countryside.

In the welcome absence of adult supervision, we did exactly as we liked, which was to join forces with the farmer's son, who lived across the road. Together we explored the woods, swam in the nearest pond, and ran between the rows of tall corn, until Mr. Frazier, the farmer, told us not to, and he meant what he said. He once spanked me with the same shingle he had used on his son.

In those days there was nothing very bad that could happen to us, except to fall out of a tree or get poison ivy. From our point of view, it was an idyllic childhood. The only hard and fast rule was to come when summoned by the clanging of a large bell that hung by the back door. When we heard it, we were to come at once, and on the whole, we did as we were told.

In our household, obedience, not cleanliness, was next to godliness. Dad, who had met our mother during the First World War, was by choice and inclination a strict Edwardian father, firm with me but harsh with my two brothers, especially the older one. And no one, including our mother, questioned his authority.

When it came time for school, I was sent to the Watertown Country Day School run by two inspired young teachers, Miss Porter and Miss Manson. Their white clapboard house had a front hall with one large room on either side and a kitchen across the back where we boiled down sap that we collected from maple trees on the property. It took such a long time that we succeeded in steaming the wallpaper off the walls. The yield was about a tablespoon per child, which we poured onto snow and ate warm.

Classes that involved reading, writing, and working out arithmetic problems were held in the two front rooms. Everything else happened out-of-doors or in the big gray barn behind the house. There was also a shed where the goat lived. To teach us responsibility, every child had to take care of the goat for a week. I remember my parents being much amused by a report card that said: "Sydney has taken her full share of the goat."

In the ample backyard, we built houses out of packing crates, jumped rope, and played games. In the barn, we were taught music by one of the parents, a classically trained opera singer, and we learned songs in French and German. We also danced on a makeshift stage at one end of the barn, performed plays that we wrote, and produced a wonderful Christmas pageant that included every student in the school. Quite recently, a classmate long retired and living in Florida sent me a photograph taken of the nativity tableau. I smiled when I noticed that the entire cast wore snow pants and galoshes under their robes. There was no heat in the barn.

I adored school, but according to report cards saved by my mother, I had trouble with spelling and reading from the start. In June 1940, one teacher wrote: "Sydney is not yet up to other members of her group in speed and fluency." Unbeknownst to anyone at the time, I was dyslexic. However, I excelled in Written Expression, and the same teacher observed that the mechanics of writing and spelling did not seem to hinder my efforts "to put ideas on paper."

By fourth grade, my reading had improved and my eager parents were happy to hear that I was "extremely creative in all the arts, especially poetry," and wrote "lovely poems far above her age and grade level." Then, as now, the poems were about pets, plants, people, and country life. I doubt that I would be a writer today had it not been for the Watertown Country Day School.

Alas, from that nurturing environment I was plunged into fifth grade in a no-nonsense school that gave neither praise nor points for "written expression," and my deficiencies in reading and spelling caused great concern. It was the beginning of a nightmare and the end of the poetry. When the results of the placement test came, I was put back into fourth grade at a different school, and the poems were driven underground, where they remained for more than seventy years.

Fast-forward through an otherwise charmed life. For forty-five years, I lived with, learned from, and loved a tall, gentle, funny Englishman. We lived in the house of our dreams, which we shared with beloved and entertaining terriers and several adopted cats; we housed, for extended periods, young relations from England; and we made a few good friends. In addition, I was able to live close to the land of my heart. I was far enough but not too far from my parents and had a teaching job that I enjoyed, with holidays and summers free to garden. Making the garden was a spontaneous response to having a piece of land and loving to be out-of-doors.

It was a wonderful life that absorbed its share of shocks and sorrow. My parents died, and my husband, Martin, was badly injured in an auto accident in 1995. His car was hit head-on by a heavy pickup truck. But after three months in the nursing home, he came home, somewhat the worse for wear because he had broken both knees and now had a pronounced limp.

For me, the accident was a wake-up call. For the first thirty-five years, I had been leaning on him. It was not obvious to most people, but he was my rock. I was like a piece of seaweed, wafting this way and that with the currents but firmly attached to my rock. I was writing, speaking, teaching, and all the while, expanding the garden. He did everything else—finances, house maintenance—and I never called a plumber or an electrician. He could do it all. After he retired, he even shopped for groceries. But now, it was my turn to take the reins. And during the next ten years, I acquired the tools I needed to live on in the house after he died.

Even then, how much I had to learn! And how much I needed those good friends. One of them was Peter Wooster, an enchanting, gifted young man whom I met through gardening. A designer of one-of-a-kind houses, he had recently been bitten by the gardening bug and was transforming a level hilltop into a fascinating one-of-a-kind garden. Starting with a generous square, he enclosed it with a weathered picket fence and divided the interior into half a dozen beds in perfect balance and immaculately edged. Immaculate is the first word I think of when I think of Peter; also witty. He has a delicious sense of humor. Within the garden's strict boundaries, he planted a smorgasbord of trees and shrubs, annuals and perennials from glamorous places where temperatures are hot, colors vivid, and the foliage large and lush. But Peter's disciplined approach to both his life and garden was what held everything together.

That discipline has been sorely taxed since 2006 when a stroke robbed this vital, brilliant man of speech, the use of his right leg, and worse still, his dominant hand. On this uneven ground, he has fought his way back to life, independence, and a new career as a collage artist, and I feel honored to be able to literally lend him a hand. Every Sunday, I show up to glue selected images onto mat board. And every Sunday when I arrive, Peter is already prepared, tools laid out on the table— scissors for trimming, glue pot and brush, brayer for rolling the pieces absolutely flat.

We talk very little. After so many Sundays, there isn't much we need to put into words, but usually I know exactly what he wants. His mind is working all the time. Mine is at rest. And it was one Sunday driving home that a handful of words came to me. They sounded like a poem, and when I reached the house, I called Peter and repeated them. He said, "Write it down." This does not sound momentous in the retelling, but for Peter every sentence is an effort, and it meant so much.

After that more words began coming, and I wrote them down. Soon I fell into the habit of waiting for words every morning and during the week shaping them into poems, which I would bring with me on Sundays. After we had finished a collage and had lunch, I would read the poem to him. He would always say, "More." And that is how this book came about. It is because of Peter and for him and for Kim Proctor, who has been the closest and staunchest of friends, with love and thanks.

Where We Walk

We walk in all seasons
and most weathers—
the dog and I.
But today rain has melted
the first snow,
and the fields are slippery.
So we take the road
that runs through a valley
carved out by the glacier
as it retreated north.
In its wake, the land
rises and falls in folds,
now awash with dormant grasses
bleached pale gold and tan.
But where a little brook
overflows its banks, the grass
is still green
with memories of summer
and the promise
of spring to come.

Circle of Life

Parallel Journeys

My friends are traveling
to Europe, China, and Vietnam
while I sit here
at the kitchen table
as I have done
each day
for so many years.

The travelers stand in groups
gazing upward
at stained glass windows
and the marble agonies of Christ.
I look out across a garden
surrounded by woodland trees,
close-set and reaching for the sun.

The wayfarers visit temples
and study the passive countenance
of Buddha.
I stay at home
and contemplate the field
that in my lifetime
has become a forest.

In ancient monuments,
my traveling friends seek beauty
and answers to the question
of who we are
while I watch the trees grow
and search within for
that glimmer of transcendent light.

Enchanted Summers

Who knows at what moment
children lose their natural intimacy
with the animals and plants
of the earth, which
for a time
they share as equals?

When I was young,
my brother and I
used to swim in ponds
as warm as blood,
the color of tea,
and abounding with wildlife.

We floated like the frogs,
our legs trailing behind us,
and afterwards picked leeches
off each other
and lay in the sun.

I remember feeling the grass
growing up through my body
and my heart beating
down into the ground.

For a few enchanted summers,
we swam and basked
the afternoons away
while time stood still,
and the months from June
to September were measureless.

Farms Long Gone

I did not fall
far from the tree
and when I drive
the country roads,
their old familiar names
echo down the years
and whisper to me still.

They tell of long gone
farms and farmland,
wet grass and bare feet,
patient work horses
in heavy harness,
and the urgency before
a summer storm
when sweating men
with pitchforks raced
against the rain.

In those days, wiry farmers
accustomed to hard labor
tossed the fragrant hay
onto a wagon,
higher and higher,
while the horses
shifted in their traces
and stomped away the flies.

Suddenly, the wind would barrel
in from the west, driving
thunderheads before it
as lightning split the sky
and sent the farmers scrambling
onto the rick.
At a slap of the reins,
the team would plunge forward,
and the wagon,
with its swaying load,
rumble toward the barn.

Carnations

I didn't see the bunches
of miniature carnations
being unpacked by the florist,
but their clove scent
transported me back in time
to Sundays when my father
would take me with him
to visit his patients
in the hospital.
Always at their bedsides
there were carnations, usually white
like the neatly folded sheets.

A red-haired Irish nurse
would soon bustle in:
"Top 'o the mornin,' doctor."
"And the same to you,"
my dad would say.
What is it about smells
that make them so evocative?
While memory retains and reproduces
events that have already happened,
scent instantly awakens
past experience as if present
in the here and now.

Awakening

I paused on the stairs
because someone touched my arm
and said:
"You will remember this moment
For the rest of your life."

I was seventeen and eager
to change my costume
for the last act
of *Our Town*, the play
that had awakened in me
a sense that what makes
us human is our incapacity
to live life fully,
"Every, every minute."

I realize now
that simply having lived
is enough—
always different, always the same,
and only once, world without end.

Tales from Childhood

As a child, I wrote
sunny stories about family life
and the pets that
shared it—dogs and cats,
a Rhode Island Red hen
who perched on the crossbeam
under our breakfast table,
and the garter snake that
slept with my younger brother.

Later, I wanted to write
about the complex relationships
I sensed but did not
fully understand between
our anxious, affectionate English mother
and our American father—
small of stature but strong willed,
a doctor accustomed to obedience,
at war with my brothers.

The task was too hard,
and I was too young.
I did not know and
could not imagine how
their lives might unfold
nor how they would end.
Now, I alone remember the
stories I will never write
and never forget.

The Fulcrum of Christmas

Every year, they begin arriving
early in December,
the Christmas cards,
ticking off the years—
first, family photos of new babies;
then, unsteady toddlers,
toothy grins in grade school,
and later, bored teen-agers
who soon leave the nest.
Now, there are graduations
and weddings, grandchildren and funerals;
families increasing at one end,
dwindling at the other
while the fulcrum of Christmas
balances the births and deaths,
triumphs and tragedies,
days and nights,
as time passes and now
becomes then.

Brothers

They are both gone now,
my two brothers, one younger,
one older, both as difficult
as they were charming,
wonderful as friends, impossible as husbands,
and as fathers, too much
like our own,
full of good cheer
but autocratic and volatile.
Nor, as men,
did the brothers get along.
They hadn't spoken in years
when the younger was diagnosed
with a serious illness.
Without a moment's hesitation,
the older brother dropped everything
and flew across the country
to be with him.
What they talked about,
I do not know,
but for the next year,
they never stopped talking.

Singing Still

When I was young
I used to roam
my father's garden
at sundown.
In summer,
bats silhouetted against
the evening sky
ricocheted through
the soft, warm air,
and as the light faded,
fireflies lit their flashing lamps.
On clear nights,
stars cast a pale radiance
over the landscape
while grasshoppers
sang from high in the trees:
Katy-did, Katy-didn't;
Katy-did, Katy-didn't.
Beyond reach
and beyond time,
they are singing still.
But I hear them now
as an old woman
in my own garden.

The Power of the Unseen

Why this sudden interest
in physics, a branch of science
I avoided as a student
out of diffidence
and fear of failure,
but now find wholly engrossing?
At breakfast, I pore over
an introduction to the subject
written for children,
its pages filled with
simple experiments.

I rub a plastic spoon
against my shirtsleeve
and delight in the way
the spoon attracts
scraps of paper.
I marvel at the phenomenon
of magnetism.
But for every puzzle solved
by science, another
takes its place.

And the more I learn
about energy and matter,
the more I am awed by
the power of the unseen.
Invisible but at the ready,
energy is all around us:
in the light and heat of the sun,
in towering thunderheads
charged with electricity,
and in the movement
of air currents as gentle
as a caress or as violent
as a tornado.

How is it that we accept
these miracles but doubt
the existence of God
or whatever great
force rules nature?

In the face of compelling
evidence that we are not
masters here, but part of
an infinite, ongoing mystery,
we cling to the physical world,
wherein lie clues to life,
the greatest miracle of all.
And there is comfort
in knowing that we have partaken
of the sun's energy
and that energy is never lost
but recycled and transformed
again and again.

Good News Café

Two old ladies having lunch,
friends of fifty years,
talk of this and that
as a patient waitress stands
beside their table.
"Soup, I think," says one;
the other nods agreement.
They always have the soup,
and after that, either shrimp
or the portobello mushroom cap
with goat cheese, followed by
apple tart, which they share.
Replete, they leave together,
parting in the parking lot,
each reassured that the other
is alive and well.

The Copper Beech

I remember when my neighbor
planted the copper beech
beside his barn, a sapling,
its stem no thicker than
the handle of a broom.
Today, its stout gray trunk
supports a magnificent bronze canopy
that spans the entire field.

The planter of the tree
died on a business trip
thirty years ago,
and the property
passed into the hands
of a new young neighbor,
who mowed around the tree
until its low-branching boughs
created a pool of shade
where no grass grew.

Now, the new neighbor,
no longer young,
looks out on a tree
whose life expectancy
far exceeds his own.
Soon, no one will remember
those who witnessed its youth.
But new generations will pause
in passing to admire
its unrivaled beauty.

Succession

On January twenty-fifth, nineteen sixty-one,
my husband and I moved
as newlyweds
into the old yellow farmhouse
where I live today,
surrounded by woodland and memories.
Martin died under this roof
ten years ago, and I
hope in due course
to do the same.

While we were young and
carrying on our busy lives,
nature in its unhurried pace
gave birth to a forest.
In a cow pasture, abandoned
long ago by the farmer
who tilled this rocky land,
evergreen junipers, the first invaders,
marched in and took
their place in the sun.

But soon, deciduous hardwoods
began to shade them out:
black birches, oaks, maples, and
beeches, whose tight pewter-gray bark
tempts boys like my older brother
to carve hearts and names
with their new jackknives.
Somewhere, my brother's handiwork remains,
forgotten love and his initials,
stretching with each passing year.

Going White

Jack Russell Terriers
have predominantly white coats
for visibility in the field.
But recently, I noticed
white hairs among the brown
of Phoebe's mask, and my
heart skipped a beat.
She's young, only seven years old,
in her prime and fully prepared
to tread upon the lion
and the adder—
a credit to the breed
that combines the blood
of whippet, beagle, and bulldog
to achieve the tough, stubborn
little clown of a dog
asleep in my lap,
where she will leave countless
white hairs on my bathrobe.

Rooted Deep

My life is small
but rooted deep
among the rocks
that define a landscape
rich in trees.
Though savage gales
have ripped off limbs,
the trees survive,
mute and stoic,
heartwood exposed,
waiting for new bark
to bind the ragged edges
of their wounds.
I, too, have felt the wind
and heard the sharp report
of breaking boughs
and now, in stillness,
wait for healing to begin.

The Territory of Age

If youth is wasted
on the young,
perhaps age is wasted
on the old.
Although politicians court us
and our votes are heard,
we remain largely silent
about the one subject
upon which we are
uniquely qualified to speak—
the inner landscape of age.
For purposes of discovery,
this familiar but often unexplored
territory bears closer scrutiny.
Having the luxury of time,
I sift through the many
layers of my life,
sorting and examining,
more amused now than critical
of the person I was
at different stages.
While the old ghosts slumber
beneath their dust sheets,
others give a last twitch
as they depart,
leaving the slate wiped clean.

Autumn Walk

An old woman with wild hair
walked a small white dog,
the leash taut between them.
The woman's gait was awkward
but quick; the dog's, light
and nimble.
Ten feet apart, they covered
the ground like leaves
carried by the wind—
two moving dots, blown across
a broad expanse of hillside
and upward to meet the horizon.

That Good Night

I want to go gentle
into that good night
and pray that my body
will not rage against mortality
but submit and merge
into the soft, thick darkness
where I have walked before
and found it less threatening
than I had feared.
But the sudden descent
had come too soon,
when death still seemed
a remote possibility,
as it always does
to the strong and fit.
I am older now,
and this time
when the day is spent
I want to welcome night
as I welcome winter
after a long, hot summer,
bequeathing to those I love
the radiant light of spring.

Gathering In

Before the written word
and long before the Greeks
explained their universe
in myth and fable,
primitive peoples
recorded what they saw.
In cave drawings of
extraordinary power and grace,
they depicted mammals
with whom they shared
the mountains and river valleys,
deserts, grasslands, and forests.
Roofed over by the distant sky,
their world extended only as far
as the eye could see.
And within these boundaries,
man and beast
spent their brief time
on earth.

I, on the other hand,
have reached my eighty-second year.
I have crossed continents and oceans
but always come back
to a clearing in the woods
where native Americans
once slipped between the trees
on silent feet
and animals still roam.
Since earliest childhood,
the natural world has been
my home and habitat,
providing food
for body and soul,

and as I round out
my long life,
I gather to me
every creature that rustles
among the fallen leaves—
the fox that passes
like a shadow
across the garden;
even the sinister coyotes
that suddenly materialize, then vanish
in plain sight.
They are part of me,
and I of them.

Morning, Noon,
and Night

The Verges of the Day

I wake up every morning
to the sun going down
in a painting
that I love
of a place where
I have walked
with the dog
since she was a pup,
where a wide green path
sweeps through acres
of tall native grasses
on either side.
Geysers of big bluestem,
already turning orange
in the mellow light of
autumn at the end
of the day,
guide us homeward
before the night falls.

Coming to Life

My mind clicks on;
the day begins.
I am awake
but not yet alive.
Life begins with commitment
to the day, this day;
the hours from sunrise to sunset,
dusk to evening,
and on into the night.
Thy will be done.
And let my will
propel me onward
through the darkness
into the light.

The Light That Makes Time Visible

To capture light in words
is no easier than
to render it in pigment,
but Monet found a way
in shimmering deconstructions
of the cathedral at Rouen,
painted at different hours
of the day
over many weeks.
Nearer home, his subjects were
haystacks and trees,
flowers and views,
his own garden
in all seasons and weathers,
year in and year out,
from dawn until dusk;
he painted the light
that makes time visible.

February Morning

On this still winter morning,
the temperature hovers near zero,
and where I sit
at the kitchen table,
a cold draft wraps itself
around my ankles.
Outside in the garden,
no sign of life disturbs
the frigid calm, nor footprint
mars the snow that lies
two feet deep on every
level plane, deeper where
the wind has swept it
over the hedge and up
against the glass doors.
A few early clouds have
given way to blue sky
and bright sun.

Now the dog and I
must head out of doors
into the sparkling chill
of this February day.

Phoebe's Round

In the morning
while I make the bed,
the reigning Jack Russell Terrier
lies across the back
of a chair,
her head thrust
through the drawn curtains.
She quivers with intensity.

Because we are surrounded
by forest,
a lot goes on here:
deer hunters rattle by
in their pickup trucks,
hikers with backpacks
ply the trails,
and she is responsible
for everything: people, vehicles, wildlife,
even the dead leaves
scurrying before the wind.

Designed with small powerful bodies,
Jack Russells have speed, stamina,
and a heightened prey drive
that more than compensates
for their stature.
They were created for
a purpose: to dispatch rodents.
No master commands them.
They know what to do.
It's bred in the bone.

But every night,
these same eager little killers
stand by your bed, whining
until you lift the covers
and they go to ground.
It is the bargain you make—
your warmth for theirs.
Finally, stretched out beside you,
they move when you move,
sigh when you sigh,
breathe when you breathe,
until the new day begins.

The Message

Most days,
the first words
are unspoken.
They racket around
inside my head.
They make sounds
but no sense
until I shut my eyes.
Then, with no way out,
these scraps of utterance
settle into the recesses
of my mind
and steep like tea.

In the leaves and buds
of the Chinese Thea tree,
gypsies predict the future.
I sip the hot brew
and listen to the present.
In the ticking
of the kitchen clock,
the hum of the refrigerator,
and the soft exhalation
of a sleeping dog,
I hear the message
that all is well today.
The words will come.

Prayer for the Gift of Words

God, let there be words.
I will wait in silence,
but let them rise up
and find me.
I love the shapes
and sounds
of the English language:
the vowels, frictionless and full,
in words like resonant, round,
roar, howl, moan, and moon.
Consonants command attention, keeping order
with pursed lips, vertical strokes,
short, sharp outcries, and expletives.

Words are the stuff of work,
of dreary emails and debates,
of financial reports and wills,
instructions for assembling furniture,
and directions to a destination.
Poems employ the same words
to make music accessible,
to rage or sing songs
of praise.
Words are a gift for which
I am ever thankful,
and I pray that they
may remain with me always.

Flash in the Pan

How is it that yesterday
I had something to say—
something urgent, cogent, wise.
Driving to the grocery store,
I felt inspired.
But somewhere between the produce
and the deli counter,
that spark flickered and died.
Like a poorly constructed fire,
it flared before sputtering out—
a flash in the pan
that failed to explode.
Thoughts and words that seemed
so promising the day before
now lie in a heap,
useless and unloved.

Birdsong

Heat settles on the garden, weighty and still.
The only signs of life are birds
going about their business.
Some of their muted calls are familiar,
but many are not.
I envy serious birders,
who recognize them
and can eavesdrop
on these intimate exchanges:
"What's for dinner?"
"Isn't it your turn to catch the flies?"

Like a red spark, the male cardinal
breaks from the shade of rhododendrons,
looping through the thick air.
Next a bustling Carolina wren arrives.
Fox-colored and a little top-heavy,
it perches on the edge of the garage roof
and in a liquid warble
repeats three descending notes
over and over again.
So the summer day begins.

Morning Light

On late summer mornings
when the sky is clear
and not a leaf stirs,
when the only sounds
are the steady hum
of crickets and the tapping
of a solitary woodpecker
on a distant tree,
it is hard to believe
that the green-gold band
of sunlight inching its way
across the lawn
is actually hurtling through
the vacuum of space
at a speed calculable
but beyond imagining.
Does it disturb the air
with noise like a giant wave
crashing on the shore?

What we perceive as silent,
motionless, and constant
is really in a state of flux.
Somewhere in the universe,
the stars we see tonight
or tomorrow or sometime
in the future
have long since
left their birthplace.
And while we sleep or work,
planets collide and stars implode,
sucked into black holes
from which there is no escape.
But we go on as before,
and I know that our planet
is still rocking and turning
because the sunlight has now
reached the edge
of the flower bed.

Ephemeron

In the evening
I walk among the daylilies
and snap off each flower,
still perfect, pristine, and poignant;
the irony of it—
so beautiful but doomed—
a lifetime that unfolds
from birth to death
in a single day.
But the sadness of parting
is assuaged by the knowledge
that tomorrow will bring
a new crop of blossoms
that will lean toward me
with upturned faces,
young and lovely,
until swift death
exacts its price,
bestowing upon daylilies
their earliest botanical name, Ephemeron.

Unimportant Things

From my post
at the kitchen table,
I watch the days unfold
and marvel at the importance
of unimportant things—
breakfasts measured out in bites
of toast, cups of tea,
and news on public radio.
One morning last week,
I learned that
an asteroid narrowly missed
our planet, streaking past us
in the night
while the snow fell,
as it has done
so often this winter—
storm after storm.
Yesterday, I had to shovel
the dog's run,
and this afternoon,
three men came with ladders
to clear ice from the gutters,
boots thumping on the roof.
They have gone now;
the house is quiet,
and the sun, sinking
behind the hills,
is tinting the treetops pink.

Now

If only we understood
the moment,
not the next, but this one,
in which the rain falls soft and straight,
disappearing into the eager grass.
Already wind is moving
the moisture-laden trees,
the sky is lighter,
and the leaves
throb with life
as sun breaks through
the thinning clouds
and time moves on.

Parade

Parades lift a certain day
out of the unfolding stream
of time and make it memorable—
our human best
offered up to the piping
and the thumping
of the fife and drum.
Girls toss their batons high
while school bands play—
earnest, comical, and fine.

The Newtown Labor Day Parade
reminds us that we are
all in this together—
young and old,
people, pets, and barnyard animals—
moving forward step by step
toward another year,
another Labor Day Parade.
This one, I will remember
most of all.

The Awful Trinity

Every poem is an attempt
to describe the indescribable
or delay for one moment
the inexorable passage of time,
and every poet, a fool
who forever sifts through dross
to find one word
that expresses the awful trinity
of truth, beauty, and pain.

The Loveliest Hours

The loveliest times of day
are sunrise and the hour
before sundown, when
the last light leaps
across the valleys
from hilltop to hilltop,
bathing whatever it touches
in molten splendor
too beautiful to last.
Thus God reveals Himself,
but sparingly,
at the break of day
and the edge of night.

Storm

Driving home last night,
I saw the storm coming,
bearing down from the north
along the Housatonic River.
The sky above was filled
with a tumult of clouds
in lurid shades of purple,
black, and yellow-green
that tossed and turned,
sending powerful charges of electricity
to the ground.
At every flash of lightning
I flinched but kept moving.

Home at last, I watched
with anxiety as the trees,
heavy laden with moisture
and in full spring leaf,
thrashed in wind gusts
of forty miles an hour.

But the worst of the storm
had passed.
Soon the wind dropped,
the air cooled,
and calm was restored
to the river valley.

One More Soft September Day

Give us one more
soft September day,
rising from the mist
and as still
as a lover's breath
held in contemplation
of the beloved.
Stave off for today
October's hard blue skies
and frost-laden nights.

This once, hang
the harvest moon
a little lower in the sky
and surround it with stars
whose orbits skim the earth.
When they fade
into dawn
and the moon sets,
then we will bend
to autumn's sword of Damocles.

Evening Walk

We walked late,
the dog and I,
taking the shortest route
straight uphill into the sky,
where a new moon emerged
from the afterglow—
a shred of burnished silver
brighter than the dying day,
and all around, the hills
turned from blue to black,
pricked with twinkling lights,
as the working world
headed home for the night.
We followed suit, our careful
footsteps making no sound
in the darkness.

Full Moon, New-Fallen Snow

Last night, moonlight drew me
from one window to another
until I found myself outside
in my bathrobe and boots,
gazing into the night sky.
By what magic had darkness
been transformed into this world
of pale clarity and light?
Snow had been falling
all day, but by evening
the storm had petered out,
leaving a foot of fresh
powder, carved by the wind
into pristine dunes and drifts,
over which a full moon
now presided with aloof dignity,
casting exquisitely detailed shadows
on the new-fallen snow.

The Garden Year

The Garden Year

Gardens are full of beginnings
and endings.
It is the same
for long-lived oaks
as for weeds that
succumb to the first frost.

What lives must also die,
making room for the new.
So, too, the white-haired gardener
must one day
put down the spade.
But not yet.

Let one more autumn
pour like honey
over the landscape,
slow and golden,
and one more Indian Summer
rekindle June.

Let there be one more
winter's dreaming
of spring primroses
and summer daylilies.
Then, perhaps—
who knows?

West Wind

Against a cloudless cerulean sky,
the bare treetops slowly bend
eastward with the prevailing wind.
It takes power to move
the heavy branches
of an eighty-foot maple tree
and time to reverse direction,
back and forth in slow motion.
On the snow-covered ground,
sudden gusts bear down upon
the house with a hollow
wailing sound and clouds
of frozen particles swirl
around corners and accumulate
in drifts as the wind
catches its breath in preparation
for the next assault upon
our clearing in the woods.

Bluebirds in Winter

The bluebirds are back!
Such a joy!
And so near the house,
not ten feet
from where I am sitting
at the kitchen table.
They come for the winterberry
and are delicately but efficiently
dismantling my Christmas decorations—
two large flower pots
filled with evergreens and branches
of our native holly, thickly set
with scarlet fruits.
These are rapidly disappearing.

But more than the berries,
I love the birds,
not just for their cobalt
plumage but for the shape
of their bodies
that would just fit
into my two cupped hands,
and for their inextricable association
with happiness.

Balancing Act

Without warmth and without color,
the winter sun stares down
with evenhanded cruelty.
In the garden, rhododendrons,
unable to draw moisture
from the frozen soil,
curl their leaves inward
to conserve water.
Nature does not leave
her creations defenseless.

In the balmy months,
moisture travels freely
from root to leaf,
passing into the atmosphere
as water vapor and oxygen.
In winter, this beneficial exchange
slows but does not cease.
Evergreens continue to lose moisture.
Thus, every cold, sunny day
takes its toll.

Survival is a balancing act.
Will spring arrive in time
to replenish the water supply?
Or will leaves begin to desiccate?
Gardeners remain optimistic
as they wait
for the ground to thaw
and watch the sky.

Restless for Spring

The dog and I are
restless for spring.
The clocks have been set
ahead, but snow still covers
the ground, and winter lingers
on and on,
blue and white day
after blue and white day.

Sunny skies tempt us out
to walk, but the windchill
sends us scuttling
back inside, the dog's
paws sore from ice and salt;
my fingers numb, nose running.
But this morning I heard
the male cardinal's mating call.

Responding to the longer hours
of daylight, he announces that
it is time to select
a nesting site before
the first day of spring,
only two weeks away.
Now, it will surely come.
The birds are never wrong.

The Month of March

I love the month
of March, when everything
is yet to be.
For a week now,
the leftover snow
has been melting by degrees.
Soon longer days will
speed its departure.

In the garden,
bare patches always appear first
under the maple trees,
whose dense, twiggy crowns limit
the amount of precipitation
that reaches the ground.

In the forest,
snow gives way early
to the solar heat from
exposed rock outcrops and along
the south side of
old fieldstone walls that run
like a recurring theme
through pastures abandoned to woodland.

And one day
as we approach
the vernal equinox,
the green frogs will emerge
from the bottom of the pond,
float to the surface,
and fill the spring air
with their raucous, joyful chorus.

Harbinger

Although the sun crossed
the equator a week ago,
signs of spring
have been few.
Piles of snow still linger
along north-facing walls,
and at night temperatures
remain near or below freezing.

Even the early-breeding wood frogs
have not yet emerged
from beneath the mud.
Usually their loud, quacking chorus
drowns out the tentative
treble of the peepers.
But only the birds sing,
undaunted and on schedule.

Killdeer have returned
to the open hilltop
where I walk the dog,
and today we watched
these relatives of the sandpiper
running in agitated circles,
emitting their plaintive cries,
while searching for open ground
where they will scrape out
a shallow nest.

The dog tugged at her leash
and we moved on.
At that moment
I heard it—the sound
for which I wait
every year: a descending series
of pure, sweet notes,
uttered by the red-winged blackbird,
proclaiming that despite the chill
spring has finally arrived.

Bountiful Spring

In April, abundant rain
fueled in the vegetable kingdom
a spirit of reckless abandon.
Every flowering tree and shrub
bloomed as never before:
apple blossom overlapping with dogwood,
pearl bush with rhododendron,
viburnum with the fringetree.
Already bushels of herbaceous peonies
have come and gone,
along with old-fashioned bearded irises,
their sweetly scented lavender flowers
lasting only a few days.
After that, but before daylilies
flood the flower beds
with sunny hues,
a cool green pause settles
over the landscape
like a deep, satisfying sigh
while garden and gardener brace
for the headlong rush of summer.

Dance of the Flowers

I wonder if the great
Thomas Stearns Eliot was
a gardener, as well as
a poet.
How else would he know
that April is, indeed,
the cruellest month?
A few mild days ago,
I transported the tender plants
from windowsills indoors
to summer homes
in pots on the terrace.

Last night I brought them
into the kitchen again,
and this morning
an inch of snow covered
the ground.
But warmer temperatures
are expected by the weekend,
and out they will go,
do-si-do, out and in,
in and out,
until all danger of frost
has passed.

Summer Rain

I am grateful for wet, green air
and dripping leaves;
for the sigh of earth,
thirst slaked by rain,
that whispers in the trees
and falls in silence.

September Too Soon

It has been a summer
of astonishing beauty,
the perfect balance
of warm and cool,
rain and sun.
Now, it is September,
too soon, too short,
too lovely to stay—
the month of ripening grains
and the last sweet corn,
fragrant Concord grapes
hanging heavy on the vines,
and early sunsets,
too soon, too short,
too lovely to stay.

Falling Leaves

Riding on the fitful winds
of autumn,
the falling leaves
are fleetingly reborn
as butterflies:
wood nymphs and sulphurs,
coppers and fritillaries.
Swept up
on a rising tide
of warm air,
they pause
and hover for a few seconds
before floating to the ground.
Then a sudden blast
of cold air
from the north and west
whisks them skyward again
in a turmoil of
yellow, orange, and brown,
spinning and spiraling,
until another shift
in the wind
sends them back to earth
in a kamikaze dive.
Motionless at last,
the shattered leaves
await the blades
of the lawn mower
that will reduce them
to mulch
for next year's garden.

Gold and Blue

In the radiant world
of autumn gold,
the blues are as blue
as the Virgin's robe
in medieval art.
At that time,
the rare and beautiful
lapis lazuli,
found only in the mountains
of Afghanistan,
was ground by hand
into a pigment
more intense and precious
than all the rest.
To the monks
toiling in their cloisters,
ultramarine meant
far beyond the sea;
and so it was
with special care
that they illuminated
manuscripts of prayers and psalms
to guide the followers
of Saint Benedict
through their days,
from dawn to dark—
from gold to blue,
the one color
completing the other.
Through art and nature
they march together,
separate but indivisible.

A Time to Sow

How sudden—this short spell
of warmth
when trees have lost
most of their leaves
and gardeners have already
felt the edge of winter.
And how welcome,
the heat of the Indian Summer
sun on our backs.

We peel off gloves
and plunge bare hands
into the earth
to plant spring-flowering bulbs,
while overhead the maples
disperse their winged samara—
outwardly brown and lifeless
but carrying within,
minute plants fully formed
and as tightly packed as parachutes,
ready to expand and grow
when the conditions are right.

For wildflowers
of the fields and roadsides,
this is the last call
to reproduce themselves.
Dogbane and milkweed
split their pods,
releasing into the wind
countless seeds attached to tufts
of silken floss,
thus spreading their species
far and wide.

In sunny open places
along fence lines,
the shagbark hickories
drop their few remaining fruits,
single, hard-shelled nuts that fall
with a sound
like heavy raindrops.
They litter the ground
beneath the tree
where they will eventually
drive down roots,
unfurl their first
pair of leaves,
and carry on the cycle of the seasons.

Autumn Equinox

The setting sun,
as pale as platinum,
glows beneath
black-bellied clouds
and throws long shadows
of the horses grazing
in a field
and of my dog and me
walking down
the open road.
By the time we complete
a loop through cornfields
and along the riverbank,
dusk will have fallen.
We are approaching
the autumn equinox,
halfway between
the longest
and the shortest
days in the year,
when the sun stands still
and the world waits.
Nights are cooler now.
The summer-warmed surface
of the earth
exhales moisture
that fills the river valley
with soft gray mist.
Overhead, the mirror moon,
near full tonight,
rises in the east.

Gold on Gold

Overhead and underfoot,
sans heat, sans flame,
the autumn glows—
gold on gold adorning maples,
bright leaves shed
on forest floor,
reflected in the passive surface
of a pond
at water's edge.

In open fields,
the bluestem grasses,
standing taller than a man,
rise up and tiger stripe
the path
with shadows black and gold
and black again
as sunset leaves
the western sky.

The Bag

I knew it would
still be there—the offensive
white plastic bag,
a fugitive
from the garbage truck,
that begs unreasonable attention
in the landscape.

This eyesore arrived
last winter
on a gust of wind
and caught on a twig
high up in the tree
at the far end
of my garden.

There it has stayed,
hopelessly out of reach
and impossible to ignore.
White, which reflects
more rays of light than
the brightest red,
gave in to summer's greenery.

But now that the leaves
have fallen,
the dreaded bag
has returned,
defiant and flapping
like a windsock
in the stiff autumnal breeze.

Unexpected Visitor

A pileated woodpecker swooped down
from the forest this morning
and alighted on the trunk
of a maple tree,
braced bolt upright
by its stiff tail feathers.
Rarely seen but often heard,
hacking out chunks of bark,
this majestic North American woodpecker
has no equal in size
or splendor, with its upswept
scarlet crest, glossy black plumage,
and in flight,
a startling glimpse of white
as it spreads its wings
and with heavy beats rises
into the chill November air.

Tipping Point

As March is to spring
so November to fall,
the seasonal tipping point
when the earth inclines either
toward the long light days
of summer or winter's darkness
or balances somewhere in between,
before heavy frost turns rooftops
white and dahlia foliage black,
and maple trees still flare
like beacons
across the wooded hills.
But sunset comes early now,
and for the first time,
drivers turn on their headlights
as they make for home.

Whiteout

Framed in the kitchen windows,
the garden and surrounding woods
are pale with falling snow.
At first it came down
hard and fine, but now
in soft clumps and clusters
as if bent upon obliterating
the footprints of yesterday
and transforming the familiar landscape
into an exotic world—
an unblemished desert
as white as milk.

New England's Finest Hour

When the earth
tilts away from the sun
and November strips the landscape
of leafy softness,
the real character
of southwestern Connecticut emerges
at its spare, unyielding best.
Skeletal trees march
in orderly ranks
up ridge after ridge
of ancient hills
that formed billions of years ago
from a seething mass
of molten rock and metal,
then gradually cooled and hardened
into deep wrinkles
and craggy peaks.

Eons passed; icecaps and glaciers
came and went, gouging out
valleys and riverbeds;
wind, rain, and snow
wore down the sharp edges;
and finally all that remains
are the low blue foothills
of the Berkshire mountains.
I see them in the distance
when I walk the dog
and face to face
in my own backyard,
where the straight trunks
of maples, oaks, and tulip trees
mount the south-facing slope
and disappear behind the crest of the first hill.
Winter is New England's
finest hour.

Winter Solstice

In the transient days
before the winter solstice,
the sun, star of stars,
source of heat and light,
describes a shallow trajectory
from horizon to horizon.
In the morning,
its fiery edge ignites treetops
and throws long shadows
on the frozen ground.
By the time the sun
reaches its zenith,
the day is half spent.
And too soon,
the drama of its setting
plays out in a tumult
of purple clouds,
breaking like surf
against the western hills.

Above them, the clear sky
changes from amethyst to amber,
and in quick succession
topaz, rose quartz, and aquamarine.
The hues are always different,
but every evening this display
holds me at the window
until all color fades
into the blue-black night.

Love, Loss, and
Moving On

The Memorial Service

The memorial service was held
in a beautiful old church
on the main street.
The Congregationalists, having outgrown
their nineteenth-century home, had moved
to a new modern church,
leaving empty the white clapboard
building with perfect proportions
and tall arched windows.
On this day, sunlight poured
down through the antique glass
over a hundred bowed heads
and a bower of forsythia,
picked that morning
from the gardens of friends.
Strains of "Love divine
all loves excelling"
filled the nave
and a hundred grateful hearts
for a man
of limitless generosity
in both spirit and deed.
He was elegant and funny,
and he was my husband.

The Yellow House

We knew what we wanted:
privacy, an old house,
and a bit of land,
somewhere to put down roots
after the nomadic years.
It was the yellow house
that beckoned to us.
Although it was the home
of our real estate agent
and not for sale,
not then, but later,
it became our home.

Before that, generations of Sanfords
had slept and made love
in the small upstairs bedrooms—
hot in the summer,
cold in winter.
Sanfords had cooked
in the huge open fireplace,
baked in the beehive oven,
and eaten in the kitchen
with the farmhands.

Sanford men had brought wives
to this house,
raised their children here,
and buried their dead
from the parlor, used only
for funerals and weddings.
I came as the bride
of a lanky, humorous Englishman.
When he died forty-five years later,
I stayed on to keep myself
And the yellow house alive.

That Morning

That morning,
when I turned my back
on death,
there were two fawns leaping
in the field,
as if his soul
had found new life.
Later, a bluebird flew low
over the garden,
pausing briefly
in the apple tree
before taking its leave
and with it, my heart.

Parting

In the beginning, I thought
I wouldn't make it
through the day.
Minutes dragged into hours
since death did us part.
But the day passed;
weeks followed,
and finally, after a year,
I half expected to hear
his voice saying,
"You've done it!
I knew you could."
But there was no sound.
In that silence,
I came to accept
his absence
as the new reality.
Only then did it begin
to get better.

Gradually, like the halting return
of spring, joy and pleasure
ventured out into the thaw.
And I realized, at last,
that if I live,
he lives.
That is reason enough
to get up every morning.

Day After Day

What was it about us
that worked?
"Why do you love me?"
I would ask,
and he would say,
"I don't know,"
which never satisfied me.
There were so many reasons
to love him:
his charm and patience,
that rare combination
of quick wit and kindness,
his boney English face,
and the way he walked.
People thought he had been
wounded in the war,
but he hadn't.
Although he was a pilot,
he survived unscathed.
I attributed his loping gait
to a tall, thin frame
loosely tacked together
that gave him
a kind of ramshackle grace.

Martin never hurried or stood
if he could sit.
He listened more than talked
and was a great reader.
We both loved language
and had dictionaries
in every room.
At breakfast,
we used to peruse
Page-a-Day word calendars.
I still find old, discolored pages
tucked into books
to mark some long forgotten place.
Studying them now,
I wonder how anyone
so present can be absent.
Day after day
I sit in his chair,
looking out across our clearing
in the woods.
It no longer matters
why he loved me,
only that he did.

The Comfort of His Clothes

Clothing is so personal that
whenever a death occurs,
well-meaning friends and family members
offer their help
in disposing of garments
that might remind the bereaved
of their loss.
But one widowed friend lived
in her husband's old sweater
for weeks, taking comfort from
its warmth and the smell
of pipe tobacco that still
clung to its fibers.

For me, it was limp
shirts with torn breast pockets
where Martin always hid treats
for the dog to find.
Now these old shirts,
washed hundreds of times,
protect me in the garden—
from sun in the morning
and mosquitoes in the evening.
I lift them from the dryer
and bury my face
in their warm folds before
hanging them in the closet.

Solitaire

It was no illusion that
we walked hand in hand.
My life began with you.
Before that I was alone,
walking the two miles home
after school along country roads;
exploring with the dog
or perched up in trees,
reading *Green Mansions* and pretending
to be the bird girl.
Being alone was not loneliness.
Loneliness came later
with the chaos and confusion.
Then, finally you.
Now I walk alone again
or sometimes with a friend,
but more often
just the dog and I,
as it used to be
but never the same
because of you,
and in the end
once more hand in hand.

Praying Hands

My husband had beautiful hands,
like the pen-and-ink study by
Albrecht Dürer, probably of the
artist's own hands—
palm to palm,
long, tapering fingers just touching
at the tips, every vein
and tendon rendered with delicate
strength and precision.
Hands like these could perform
string tricks for children,
assemble complex machinery,
and tease apart stubborn knots.
They once held mine
and caressed my body as
never before and never again.

The Price of Being Alive

When does it go away?
The pain, not the loving—
love goes on beyond time
and without end.
But it has been years
since my husband's death,
and still pain runs
through the secret passages
of my heart, springing up
when least expected.
In the house we share—
pain and love and I—
we move as one,
and the more familiar
I become with my companions,
the more I believe them
to be opposite faces
of the same coin,
the inescapable price
of being alive.

Certain Times

The other day,
it was a ceramic rabbit
that caused the familiar
stab of pain.
It had been a joke,
and I fell for it.
The rabbit was convincing enough
to send me flying out
into the garden,
ranting and raving and waving
my arms while he laughed.
Another time,
his distinctive handwriting
on an old envelope
will stop my heart beating
and let the unbearable sorrow
fill a reservoir within me.
Should the floodgates ever fail,
I would surely drown.

The Days Between

It is almost as if
I had welcomed back
the acute pain of loss;
as if clinging to it
could bind him to me.
Perhaps if I could have
loved more deeply,
he would not have died.
My mind has been filled
with irrational thoughts
since the anniversary
of my husband's death.
Is this normal
after so many years?
I know in my heart
that whether it is
or is not doesn't matter.
Life begins, and life ends.
The days between
are what count.

Summing Up

In the ten years since
Martin's death, I have cobbled
together a new life—
writing articles and a book,
putting to sleep
one little terrier, raising another;
discovering the depths of friendship
and the pleasures of solitude;
all the while thinking that
if I just kept going
everything would be all right.
And it was, until suddenly
the ground gave way.
I had never heard of
catatonic depression.
Now, I have.
And it has meant starting
over, one foot in front
of the other, and that
is why I walk
every day.

In the Dark

There was no loud explosion,
only silence and the sensation
of being slowly sucked into
a whirlpool of impenetrable darkness.

Pressed back by centrifugal force,
no walls came crashing down.
But just beyond my reach,
their rotary motion carved out
a prison of endless night.

There, stripped of all identity,
I became one of countless
particles of matter,
doomed for eternity to circle
an invisible axis.

Above me, time passed;
life went on;
the sun shone or didn't,
it rained,
and the first snow fell.

Sometime after that,
I sensed rather than saw
the pale shaft of sunlight
and turning toward it,
began the long ascent.

Walking Out

All I can remember now
is walking and walking and
walking; up and down halls
all exactly alike except for
the numbers on the doors,
and at the nurses' station,
different faces every eight hours.
I don't remember my visitors
although I know they came,
bringing me news I can't
recall, and food I may
or may not have eaten;
flowers that soon shriveled up
in the dry, overheated room
where I lay, unresponsive
I am told,
until one day was different.
But even that day has
slipped away with the others.
All I know is that
I kept walking.
It was the way out.

Eternal April

This spring, so long delayed,
emerges like a stone rubbing—
gradually from the mist, where
warmer air meets the snow
still lying in patches
on the winter-weary ground.

Yesterday, the dog and I
were startled by the shrill
cries of killdeer returning to
their hilltop nesting sites.
Soon, the peepers' sleigh-bell chorus
will ring in the season.

I hear these joyful sounds
and watch the snow melt
with mixed emotions.
Martin died in April
ten years ago, but love
and longing bloom every spring.

Battles Great And Small

In my small world,
it has been a year
since a handful of words
came to me unbidden
and from a source
of which I was unaware
that expressed my fervent gratitude
to be alive, having survived
a private battle with depression.

On the world stage,
June two thousand and fourteen marked
the seventieth anniversary
of great battles
on the beaches of Normandy
that, despite staggering losses,
gave the Allies a foothold
in Europe and ultimately
victory over Nazi Germany.

My older brother was there;
my shambling, absent-minded sibling
who hated organized sports
and lived to play jazz
on his second-hand clarinet.
Days before his nineteenth birthday,
he scrambled down swaying ropes
into the surf and struggled
toward Utah Beach.

Later, in the foreign darkness,
survivors of his unit regrouped
for a pre-dawn advance
across open fields
where the hedgerows bristled
with well-hidden enemy guns.
In an eerie pause between explosions,
my brother heard his name:
"Hey, Webber, good luck
and happy birthday!"

By the end of that day,
my brother was headed back
across the Channel
on a stretcher
among all the other stretchers
bound for England and safety.
He told me this story
as an old man,
still tormented by survivor guilt.
"I've always wondered," he said,
"what happened to that guy."

Where Love Remains

Today, as I drove past
the house where my husband
once lived,
where we first met,
I felt again
for one instant
that sudden stab
of joy and pain,
of love, ill-timed
but all consuming,
infinitely sweet but terrifying.
Swiftly, the house
and the moment
passed into memory,
where that love remains,
burning like a fire,
warming the empty room
of my heart.

Peace

When I flung wide the doors
of a closely guarded life,
kindness and new friendships
rushed in to comfort and divert.
But when the tide is low,
the surge withdraws,
revealing shards of
broken heart imbedded in the sand,
and in the distance,
the long line of the horizon
where I have found
that peace which passeth understanding.

Acknowledgments

My editor, Lorraine Anderson, helped me see a book of poetry in what had simply been a stack of poems. For this insight alone, she would have been worth her weight in gold, but she has also exhibited extraordinary patience and sensitivity in bringing this book to life, sharing my joys and woes along the way. Thank you for everything, Lorraine.

Graphic designer and illustrator Barbara Cottingham is responsible for the physical appearance of the book, its cover and interior. I knew how it should feel but Barb knew how it should look in order to capture that feeling, which she has done with grace and elegance. A thousand thanks.

Fine artist, printmaker, and photographer Kimberly Day Proctor took the cover photo of the place that gave the book its title and the back cover photo of vintage farm equipment with vintage poet and dog. In addition, Kim has been an unflagging source of moral support and a frequent walking companion.

Family members and many kind friends have provided encouragement and lent an ear to new poems. Grateful thanks to my two sisters-in-law, Marianna Webber and Nancy Webber, and my niece, Jeni Webber, and to dear friends: Anne Harrigan, Kathy Kling, Lee Anne White, Barbara Bixby, Patricia Laurans, Marilyn Rennegal, and Andrea Zimmermann. I have also been buoyed up by enthusiastic emails from my late husband's niece, Sara Woodall, author of *Voices from a Trunk: The Lost Lives of the Quaker Eddisons*.

Sydney Eddison lives with her Jack Russell Terrier, Phoebe, in a yellow farmhouse surrounded by a 2½-acre garden of her own creation in Newtown, Connecticut. Her articles have appeared in publications such as *Fine Gardening* and *Horticulture*, and she is the award-winning author of seven books on gardening, including *Gardening for a Lifetime, A Passion for Daylilies,* and *A Patchwork Garden*. This is her first book of poetry.

Made in the USA
Middletown, DE
31 August 2015